GET THAT GIRL YOU WANT

How To Make Her Fall Helplessly For You

By

Noah Scott

Table of contents

Introduction

Chapter 1

Chapter 2

Chapter 3

- ☒ Maintain her interest between dates
- ☒ Make it official
- ☒ Allow your confidence to develop naturally as you gain experience

Conclusion

INTRODUCTION

You will soon understand how to get a girlfriend by becoming her obvious choice, so the girl you like will choose you over everyone else chasing her.

There's no bullish*t as "more confident" or "talking to more girls" here.

Only 20 proven techniques you can apply to attract the girl you like and make her your girlfriend.

How To Get A Girlfriend
Chapter 1

1. Meeting Ladies

Stop attempting to find a girlfriend

As contradictory as this may sound, it's the first step toward getting a girlfriend. Stop trying, instead, get in each interaction you have got with ladies expecting nothing in return. You'll be stunned by how "not giving a shit" will result in ladies chasing you.

Most men will give their very best to please ladies into liking them, yet men who don't put in the effort to impress ladies, stand apart like a rose among thorns.

Ladies love challenges, so when a person who won't hesitate to express his genuine thoughts and even contradict her, comes along, he becomes the person worth talking to.

2. Make her notice you

Be fashionable. Wear clothes and jewelry that draw in ladies and begin discussions. Leather jackets and well-tailored suits are good for a start. If you've always wanted a tattoo, you can go ahead and get it.

Anything you can do to shake things up from how you introduce yourself will make all the difference in drawing in an entirely different rush of female attraction.

3. Get ready to move toward her

Before you approach her, dispose of whatever other reasons that are holding you back, for instance, expecting she simply ain't interested in you assuming you've never had a girlfriend

Such limiting assumptions will not get you anywhere.

This is the way to re-think a few normal negative reasons with positive motivations to Make a move!

For instance:

"It's pointless talking to her because she won't be interested in me" = "I should go talk to her because she appears bored."

"She's outside my league" = "I wonder whether she's cool enough to hang out with?"

This will enable you to approach girls you like in a positive manner, and you'll inevitably turn into a guy who is really desirable to be around.

4. Be confident when approaching her

Now that you're prepared, go ahead and approach her. Smile, loosen up your body language, and approach in a non-confrontational manner, similar to how you'd ask a shelf stacker where the butter is in a mall.

Watch your voice when you speak to her to ensure that it isn't too high and obnoxious, as it would be if you were a beggar asking for money. The word "pardon me" in particular is a desperate request that no one can take coming from a stranger. That's a huge turnoff.

Use a normal or downwards vocal inflection rather. You're in luck if you have a voice like Vin Diesel's.

Make sure to maintain your smile and lean slightly back when speaking to her to avoid being all up in her face. Maintain eye contact and explain why you had to stop by to say hello.

A sincere compliment is the most effective approach to accomplish this.

5. Offer her a sincere compliment

Tell her precisely why you moved toward her and be as specific as possible. Utilize the principal thing you saw about her that pulled you in. Maybe it's her charming grin, her dimples, or on the other hand if you see her a lot perhaps this time her hair is tied back interestingly.

Give her an honest compliment.

If she's a stranger and you run into her during the day, say, "Hey, I know this is random, but I just strolled past you and thought I had to go back and talk to that girl."

However, there's no need to bring up any awkwardness if you run into her in a bar. It's Ok to say "Hello" or "Hi, I noticed you from across the bar."

6. Tease her

Tease is the simplest method for making sexual pressure between you and a lady you like. Begin teasing ladies consistently.

Teasing a lady

For instance, on the off chance that a lady says she loves cats you can say "Hold on... you're a cat lady? How many cats do you own? If by chance it's more than 9 we ain't gonna work out".

In the brief moment, it takes for her to acknowledge you're simply teasing (and not offending her) she encounters a monstrous sensation of euphoric relief. That feeling is typically joined by giggling and perhaps a punch on the arm for you if you're lucky.

The more you tease ladies and give them that little tension to ease "high", the more they'll become drawn because when you courageously tease ladies it sends them a subconscious message that your genes are fantastic.

It shows her you're not scared of gambling with a conflict and that she can depend on you to adhere to your beliefs and be honest. You're a defender, not a sucker.

Chances for teasing will happen normally when you adhere to your opinion and stop faking agreeing with ladies to satisfy them constantly.

Continuously be paying special attention to cute things she says or does so you can bring them up as being adorable or entertaining.

7. Center your conversation on her

Pay attention to her and make her the center of your discussion. You'll set out countless chances for teasing her and you won't ever be lost for discussion subjects.

Center your conversation on her

It's a well-known fact that young ladies like men who pay attention to them so give her what she needs: Your ears.

At the point when the emphasis is on her, you leave substantially less room for mistakes from your side, in addition, it offers you a lot of chances to tease her because she personally presented material to you on a plate.

What made you pick this table? No, you picked it since you saw me sitting here!
What brings you to the park? Oh, I thought you were scavenging for food in the trash cans!
Why don't you like dogs? You're definitely a cat lady. Assume she has twelve cats.

When you can't help contradicting something or find something she says charming you can say "I don't think you and I will get along", or something comparable.

She'll leave the discussion thinking "that man is lots of fun" when talking to herself. Yet, remember, you mustn't let her leave until you get her number!

8. Get her number

At that point when you feel the conversation has reached a climax, make excuses to leave and get her phone number.

Getting a lady's number

Regardless of whether you're in a bar and she's not going anywhere it's in every case good to go join your mates and give her some space so she rejoins her companions and fills them in regarding you.

Odds are later in the night she'll come to find you once more and you can take things further.

This Is known as the push-pull impact. It's consistently vital to pull back a little in any new collaboration so she doesn't get worried that you're never going to leave.

To get her number just give her your phone and tell her you'll message her.

Chapter 2
Going On Dates
Texting a lady in-bed

9. Invite her on a date

Avoid attempting to accomplish everything in a single text. Build up her excitement, comfort, and intrigue about meeting up with you before inviting her on a date.

Insinuating the idea of a date first is a simple approach to naturally control the conversation towards one.

Maybe you meet her in a café and she's an espresso addict? Then you can bring up some brand-new café that's opening up soon.

Then just assembled the two things a propose it's time you go look at that new bistro together, for example

Then simply combine the two and offer that you should check out that new café with me, for example.

Step by step instructions to text a lady and ask her out

There are certain guidelines and etiquette for texting, however, these key reminders will help you stay on the right track when you're texting a female you like:

- Text and forget it- do not overthink things. After you text her, carry on with your day, and don't over text if she takes a while to respond.

- Keep it positive- if your message doesn't make you smile or laugh then, don't text it.

- Be energetic - texting is for flirting and setting up dates, not for serious and dull discussion. She needs a partner, not a friend.

- End the discussion - always put a stop to the discussion when it is at its best. It's smarter to leave her at the tip of her seat than drive things beyond that and risk turning into her text pal.

10. Location for a date

Pick a place where you can engage in activities that will make you physically intimate. For the first date, stay away from dinner dates. They are uncomfortable, pricey, and far too formal.

zoo date

If she insists on dinner, though, make sure you either offer to split the bill or say, "I'll order this, and you can grab the drinks later." She won't be able to refuse if she is a strong advocate for equal rights.

What sort of setting is ideal for a first date?

Zoos are extraordinary because you never run out of discussion subjects and activities to do. She'll snatch you when she sees an adorable creature or a terrifying one and after you've seen many various creatures it seems like you've traveled the planet together, so there's this distorted feeling that you have known one another for a very long period.

Engage in feeding the animals, giraffes, elephants, and goats. It's a ton of fun and on the off chance that she's agreeable around you, she'll grip you a lot if she feels at ease around you, which is wonderful!

Other good places for intimacy are Hookah bars, bars as a general, arcades, and ten-pin bowling.

The movie is acceptable briefly date yet not really for a first date. You can't talk, it's off-kilter as f*ck and pretty torturing since the sum total of your thoughts is taking action, and if nothing's occurred when the credits roll you leave feeling like a lead swell.

A second date can go to the movies, but not the first. You can't talk, which is both awkward and upsetting. All you can think about is making a move, and if nothing happens by the time the credits roll, you walk out feeling like a lead balloon.

11. On the date, start praising her

Ladies can go through hours picking a dress, putting on cosmetics, and doing their hair for the first date. She's done this for you to remember to show your appreciation with a sincere compliment.

"wow... you look wonderful".

12. Have high standards

Having high standards of people tells them that you are of high status and not a weakling. This is extremely alluring to ladies since it shows them you regard and love yourself. You are confident in yourself and are adamant about getting what you want.

Calling her out if she is late for the date is a terrific approach to highlight this attractive quality, like in the following example:

late for date

Because of it, she will respect you more and remember to never do it again. She'll certainly even kiss you afterward to make up for her delay!

A man of great worth will treat women with respect, be a proper gent, and treat all people with respect. Open doors for her, assist her in sitting down and act chivalrously excessive. By tipping waiters or bar staff, you can convey your concern for her and other people.

To gain respect, you must first earn it.

13. Discussion subjects to stay away from on dates

On the date, avoid talking about any of these 7 topics at all costs. These seven subjects are particularly harmful since they damage the atmosphere and spark debate rather than chemistry.

try not to talk about politics on the first date

- Discussing exes or ladies who've slipped through your fingers- Assuming you're negative about previous encounters with ladies you'll sound bitter. If you're positive you'll seem as though you're actually longing for somebody. Regardless, it's best you stay away from discussing "lost lover" totally.

- Boasting about how rich you are - only gold diggers are interested in the number of cars you have. Women of top quality will recognize boasting for what it is: a shallow approach to impress others and win their favor.

- Complaining about your job- Any discussion of your work is typically exhausting and negative. Oh, and save any disdain for your work or your boss to yourself. Nobody needs to hear it.

- Religion - Don't go there except if your main goal is to turn into a celibate monk.

- Cash - Save it for the bank. Rather than cash talk, discuss your life objectives.

- Politics - politics and trending topics lead to heated conversations and discussions. Would you like to debate and drop out or would you like to rotate and make out? See what I did there?

- Negative and toxic relationships- Once more, don't bring drama to the date, put discussions of toxic relationships in the garbage where they should be.

- "Where do you see this going?" -The purpose of a first date isn't to negotiate the conditions of your future relationship and sign a contract. They're about living in the moment, so save questions that set her in an awkward position like "what are you searching for?".

By being yourself, you can make her like you

You might not be aware of it, but the reason you haven't been able to figure out how to get a girlfriend is that you are not yourself around the ladies you find attractive.

14. By being yourself, you can make her like you.

Let me say that again:

When you are around the woman you like, you are not yourself.

We've talked about plenty of things that switch ladies off and one of your biggest "A-HA!" experiences while reading this book was probably realizing that you've always tried to win over women.

You've stayed away from an encounter, you've abstained from teasing and you've never felt confident in expressing your genuine burning sexual attraction to the young lady you're interested in.

When you fully get this, the waters will divide, the wine will turn to water, and you will be able to cross the great gates of heaven and enter the land of milk and honey by walking on water!

15. Try physical flirting with her

When you quit stressing over the result with each young lady you meet, loosen up, and have a great time, Physical flirting will begin to occur naturally!

Sitting next to her, flirting

I suggested going on dates in places where possibilities for physical touch naturally arise earlier.

If you're stressed over a lady's response to you touching her, begin with these start baby steps:

- Brush something out of her hair yet deliberately touch her neck with the palm of your hand

- If you're sitting close to her, rest your hand close to her closest leg and contact her outer thigh with your little finger
- Give her a high-five and lock your fingers for a split second before releasing her.
- When she teases you, hit her on the arm or gently push her away from you.

Assuming that her response is positive you can expand the times you touch her, if her reaction is negative, pull away and attempt some other time.

You'll know she's agreeable about actual contact when she begins giving it back to you, such as resting on your arm, snatching your hand, playfully pushing you, and so on.

These are all obvious signs that she is both relaxed and, more importantly, allured to you!

Once you're positive that she's responding to your flirting, it's time to make things official and kiss her to end all sexual tension.

Chapter 3
Sealing the deal

16. Take action and kiss her

It is your role to approach her and kiss her as soon as you notice that she is interested in you since ladies prefer to be intensely desired rather than rationally considered.

Here are a few different signs to search for just to be certain you will not get rejected when you take action:

- She fiddles with her hair while she is speaking to you
- She continues to check your lips out
- She chuckles at every one of your jokes (regardless of whether they're not amusing)
- Instead of you leaning into her, she leans in close to hear what you have to say.

Trust me, these are radiant green lights indicating she wants you to kiss her.

When you make your move, don't rush into it, let it happen when there's a short delay in the discussion and you're both looking into one another's eyes.

When you're both smiling, very close to one another (maybe even touching), and her gaze swiftly flickers from your eyes to your lips, you'll know the time is right.

Even if she declines your attempts the first time, she will appreciate you for having the guts to try, and she is likely to accept them the second time.

That is the thing, the problem of most men is that they give up after being rejected once. This is a typical rookie error because she likely wanted to kiss you but you either misread the situation and rushed it, she wasn't ready and it caught her off guard, or she felt awkward about it.

Whatever the case, the more times you try, the better you'll get at assessing the situation.

Avoid attempting to control her.

17. Do not attempt to secure a second date

At the end of the date say"Tonight was fun, we should do it again sometime," you kiss her on the cheek as you part ways on your first date.

Make her curious about what you mean by "sometime" to keep her interested.

Don't give too much away when you first start dating because women enjoy a challenge just as much as men do. If you do, the excitement of the chase will be lost, and she will quickly lose interest.

18. Maintain her interest between dates

Make her curious about you, avoid being available all the time, and flirt with the future to keep her interested in you in between dates.

At the point when you're free and text her back quickly every time it'll cause her to think you do not have anything else happening in your life.

Even if she appears angry or disappointed with you, she doesn't believe you should put her first. This is particularly true if you are only "kinda dating" and haven't made an emotional commitment to a relationship. e.g

mission-text-example

The less accessible you are, the more inquisitive she'll get, and as opposed to addressing a young lady's inquiries "matter of reality" you ought to expect to answer in a fun-loving manner that keeps her inquisitive about you, for example;

The less accessible you are, the more interested she will get, thus instead of responding to a girl's questions "matter-of-factly," try to respond in a fun way that keeps her interested in you, for example

How to respond when a female texts you and asks what you do

The more you keep her pondering about you, the more she'll want to go on another date with you.

This is the perfect way to make a girl completely obsessed with you.

By remaining jokey and excluding yourself from anything serious you will keep her pondering you.

reclude yourself from anything serious

Since displaying your emotional attachment to a lady too soon is a sure-fire method for getting a friend-zoned.

Try not to misunderstand me, It's alright to tell a young lady you love her and miss her when you're finally together, however NEVER in the beginning phases of dating.

That is because ladies will run a mile on the off chance that they sense you are more genuinely joined to them than they are to you.

This is since women will run if they think you have a stronger emotional bond with them than they do.

The method for showing a lady how much you care for her - without revealing your feelings and frightening her off - is to express your sexual admiration for her.

I miss you = I can't get over how stunning you were in that black outfit. What charming outfit are you planning to wear to our upcoming meeting?

I can't get you out of my mind = Is it strange that the rear of a Renault Megan just reminded me of how great your ass looked last night?

I need to see you again soon = So when am I going to rejoin your hot ass? Friday is looking great

I like you = I was so astonished by you last night that I might think about giving you some needles at my crack den.

I love you = I feel like I could enjoy myself in HELL with you.

19. Make it official

While you're dating a lady you truly like, it's not difficult to fall into the "Let's make things official" trap and attempt to make things official verbally.

This is how it works:

You begin to like a lady, so you want to spend a longer time with her. Your commitment to that future with her grows along with your affections for her.

You are so anxious and apprehensive about her because of how badly you want to be her boyfriend. Additionally, you begin to feel a little possessive.

You then begin to look for methods to "seal" the future. You attempt to persuade her to commit to a plan... You make a subtle suggestion about how much you care for her. You might even ask her directly how she feels about you.

I'm sure you don't need me to tell you that NONE of this is appealing to a lady.

However, it's unusual because when you like a woman, it feels exceptionally normal to do this stuff.

So what is the answer?

Indeed, it's easy yet perplexing.

At the point when you're with her, you center around having a great time as you can while you're together… and making an effort not to affirm anything or lock anything down.

Consider it: assuming you have some good times whenever you first spend time with somebody… Wouldn't it be nice to see them again?

Wouldn't it be simple to get into a relationship with them if things just kept going well and you enjoyed yourself every time you hung out?

However, if they acted nervously the entire time and pushed you to spend more time with them... You could only do that if you were feeling guilty.

I'm sorry to say it, but remorse does not win girls over.

So, whenever you're together, always keep in mind to enjoy the moment and concentrate on smiling and making her happy.

You can tease her about future meet-ups, but don't start locking her down while you're with her. To keep it open-ended, just add the term "sometimes."

Being a couple should come effortlessly after a couple of dates. Never push it.

20. Allow your confidence to develop naturally as you gain experience

There is one more crucial point I need to make on how to gradually acquire confidence before you go out and apply this instruction to get the lady of your dreams.

There is little doubt that for women, confidence is like crack cocaine.

Because of this, I must strongly advise you to act and put everything you've just learned into reality because, once you do, your confidence will grow on its own:

- Assuming that every female is interested in you
- Defending yourself
- Taking chances
- …And increasing your flirting with girls you find attractive.

Conclusion

Wrapping it up
It was very fun putting this "how to get a girl" book together. I want to believe that you get a ton of significant worth from it and use it to get the girlfriend of your dreams.

Rome wasn't constructed in a day, so if you're serious about finding a partner, you need to set your priorities straight because that shouldn't be your major focus.

No

You should invest in something far, Undeniably more important than that:

You

Because the girls you want will naturally get drawn toward you once you stop putting others on a pedestal, stop allowing people to step over the line with you, and stop caring what others think.

You'll begin to give the impression that you don't need women to be accomplished. You'll take more chances, find approaching and having a conversation with girls less intimidating, and you won't be concerned about the consequences.

You'll start to realize that getting a girlfriend isn't the most important thing in the world; it's more like a bonus for your already awesome life.

Ladies are attracted to men who believe in themselves. Who can say what they desire? Who don't let other people control their decisions and behaviors and who lead lives they are glad of.

None of this calls for you to completely change who you are.

All it requires is knowing what your identity is, what you need, and pursuing it.

That is how you excel in life and also how you find a girlfriend.

Printed in Great Britain
by Amazon

20662162R10020